Saint Simon's Island Cooks

By
Leslie Delaney
Saint Simon's Publishing Co.

Featuring Favorite Recipes From The Chefs at
Café Frederica
Chelsea
Delaney's Bistro
Halyards
Low Country Favorites

Saint Simon's Island Cooks

Leslie Delaney
Saint Simon's Publishing

Second Printing, December 2000

ISBN: 0-9671690-0-3

Printed in the USA by

WIMMER

The Wimmer Companies

Memphis

1-800-548-2537

Introduction

This is a small cookbook with a big mission. Our goal is to tell you about some of the best local restaurants and eateries on Saint Simon's Island along with some of the local scenery that inspired the cuisine and casual dining of each restaurant.

On Saint Simon's one will work up a big appetite by antique shopping, visiting the local historical sites, playing golf, or just walking on the beach and enjoying the sun.

This has been a rewarding journey to introduce local restaurants and their chefs to you, so that you can bring home a taste of the Island's good food and great hospitality. We will never forget the local clientele who have always been loyal and supportive of our restaurants.

We hope that this book brings delight and joy to our friends and visitors on Saint Simon's Island.

Table of Contents

Saint Simon's Island Lighthouse

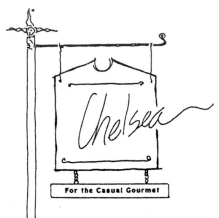

Chelsea was opened by Jeff Davis in 1987 and very quickly became an Island Favorite, featuring creative new seafood dishes and a warm casual atmosphere.

The restaurant was purchased by Jim Harford, the current owner, in 1990, and has continued to grow steadily every year through a significant expansion of the menu. With many hot and cold appetizers, as well as poultry, meat and pasta entrées, Chelsea is truly home for the casual gourmet.

Along with the catch of the day, prime rib and Romano crusted chicken on angel hair, several nightly specials have become signature dishes. Chelsea boasts that its key lime pie, with Colorado and Virginia origins, is the best in the universe.

The Pettingill brothers, Stephen, the current chef, and Kevin, the sous chef, as well as Lance Williams, Current Chef/Manager of Latitude 31, have contributed mightily to Chelsea's strong results.

Debbie Pruett, General Manager since 1992 and an employee since Chelsea opened its doors in 1987, is the spark plug that makes it all work. Debbie, Grace, Jody and their staff have a commitment to the customer, and to making everyone enjoy dinner in a comfortable setting, an extension of their living room.

Spring Carrot Puree Soup

15 large carrots, sliced	1 gallon water
1 medium-size white onion, diced	½ cup chicken base
½ cup clarified butter	Cornstarch mixed with cold water
1 cup white wine	Salt and pepper to taste
1 quart orange juice	

Sauté carrot and onion in butter in a large pot until tender. Deglaze pot with white wine. Add orange juice, water and chicken base and cook until reduced by half. Remove from heat. Strain vegetables, reserving broth. Puree vegetables. Combine puree and broth and bring to a boil. Add cornstarch mixture and cook and stir until thickened to desired consistency. Season as needed with salt and pepper.

Yield: 8 to 10 servings

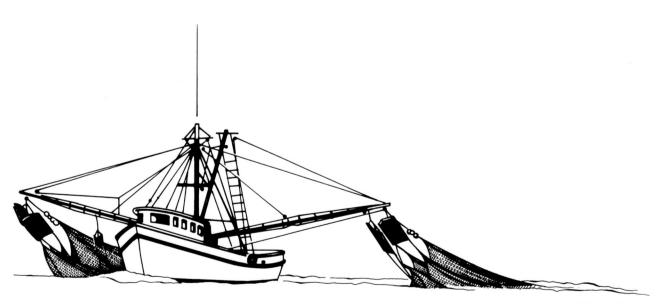

Artwork by Jennifer Smith

Kahlúa Roasted Walnut Salad with Balsamic Dressing

SALAD

½   cup warm water
1   teaspoon ham base
½   cup Kahlúa
    Salt and pepper to taste
1   cup walnuts

1   pound mixed spring greens
2   tablespoons chopped fresh oregano
2   tablespoons chopped fresh basil
1   cup thinly sliced apple

BALSAMIC DRESSING

1   cup balsamic vinegar
1   cup honey
¾   cup Dijon mustard

¼   cup sesame oil
½   cup salad oil
    Salt and pepper to taste

Combine Kahlúa, warm water, ham base, salt and pepper. Add walnuts and marinate for about 30 minutes. Discard marinade and roast walnuts at 350° for 5 minutes or until brown. Cool and chop. Combine walnuts with greens, oregano, basil and apple. To prepare dressing, combine vinegar, honey and mustard. Whisk in oils and season with salt and pepper. When ready to serve, toss salad with desired amount of dressing.

Yield: 4 to 6 servings

Goat Cheese Appetizer with Basil Vinaigrette

APPETIZER

1	pound mixed spring greens
8	ounces goat cheese
5	ounces capers
2	red bell peppers, roasted, peeled and julienne
1	medium-size red onion, diced
30	crackers of choice
1½	cups basil vinaigrette dressing

BASIL VINAIGRETTE DRESSING

¼	cup chopped fresh basil
½	cup red wine vinegar
¼	cup Dijon mustard
1	teaspoon finely chopped shallots
1	teaspoon black pepper
1	teaspoon salt
2	cups salad oil

Divide spring greens among individual serving plates. Arrange goat cheese, capers, bell pepper, onion and crackers around the greens. Top with dressing. To prepare dressing, place basil and vinegar in a medium mixing bowl. Allow to sit at room temperature for 30 minutes. Add remaining ingredients. Whisk together until thickened.

Yield: 4 to 6 servings

Spinach Salad

Salad

1½ pounds fresh spinach, washed and stemmed
1 (14-ounce) can hearts of palm, drained
1 (14-ounce) can artichoke hearts, drained and sliced
1 cup sliced shiitake mushrooms

1 cucumber, peeled and sliced
3 plum tomatoes, quartered
6 slices smoked bacon, cooked and chopped
2 cups grated mozzarella cheese
1½ cups Gorgonzola dressing

Gorgonzola Dressing

4 cups mayonnaise
1 cup sour cream
¼ cup diced yellow onion
2 teaspoons chopped garlic
2 teaspoons red wine vinegar

¼ cup chopped parsley
¼ cup chopped scallions
1 teaspoon Worcestershire sauce
½ pound Gorgonzola cheese, crumbled

Combine spinach, hearts of palm, artichoke hearts, mushrooms, cucumber, tomato and bacon. Toss well and top with cheese. Drizzle dressing over top. To prepare dressing, combine all ingredients and blend well.

Yield: 4 to 6 servings

Rice Fried Giant Sea Scallops
with Jalapeño Tomato Coulis

COULIS

2	jalapeño peppers, roasted and seeded	½	teaspoon chili powder
10	plum tomatoes, roasted and peeled	1	tablespoon salt
½	small white onion	½	tablespoon pepper
2	teaspoon ground cumin	4	cups tomato juice
½	teaspoon cayenne pepper	¼	cup vinegar

SEA SCALLOPS

1¼	pounds giant sea scallops	8	egg yolks, beaten
1½	cups flour	5	cups cooked white rice
	Salt and pepper to taste		

Combine all coulis ingredients in a blender or food processor and puree. When ready to serve, dust scallops in flour seasoned with salt and pepper. Dip in egg yolk and then coat with rice. Deep-fry at 375° until golden brown. Serve with coulis.

Yield: 4 to 6 servings

Romano Crusted Shrimp

SUN-DRIED TOMATO AND BASIL CREAM SAUCE

5 cups heavy cream
¾ cup julienne sun-dried tomato
¼ cup julienne fresh basil

1 teaspoon chicken base
   Salt and pepper to taste

SHRIMP

2 pounds (16/20 count) shrimp, peeled and
      deveined
   Flour for dusting
   Salt and pepper to taste
2½ cups Romano cheese

2½ cups breadcrumbs
3 eggs, beaten
2 cups milk
   Angel hair pasta, cooked al dente

Combine cream, tomato, basil and chicken base in a saucepan. Season with salt and pepper. Cook until reduced to desired consistency. To prepare shrimp, dust shrimp in flour seasoned with salt and pepper. Combine cheese and breadcrumbs in a shallow dish. In separate bowl, combine eggs, milk and dip shrimp in egg wash, then coat with breadcrumb mixture. Deep-fry 6 to 8 minutes. Serve over angel hair pasta and top with cream sauce.

Pistachio Crusted Snapper
with Gorgonzola Cream

SNAPPER

3	cups breadcrumbs		3	eggs, beaten
1	cup chopped pistachio nuts		2	cups milk
2	tablespoons finely chopped fresh thyme		4-6	(7-ounce) snapper fillets
½	tablespoon black pepper		1	cup olive oil
½	tablespoon salt			

SAUCE

1	small white onion, diced		1	tablespoon chopped garlic
½	tablespoon salt		½	tablespoon seafood base
	Black pepper to taste		3	cups heavy cream
¾	cup red wine		½	cup crumbled Gorgonzola cheese
2	tablespoons Worcestershire sauce		2	tablespoons chopped scallions

Combine breadcrumbs, nuts, thyme, pepper and salt in a shallow dish. Combine egg and milk in a separate dish for an egg wash. Dust snapper fillets with breadcrumb mixture, dip in egg wash, and then roll in seasoned flour. Sauté fillets in olive oil until golden brown. To prepare sauce, sauté onion in a skillet. Season with salt and pepper. Deglaze skillet with red wine. Add Worcestershire sauce, garlic and seafood base. Cook until reduced to ¼ cup. Add cream and reduce to desired consistency. Stir in cheese and scallions. Serve sauce over fillets.

Yield: 4 to 6 servings

Rack of Lamb with Roasted Garlic Rosemary Glacé

LAMB

4-6	(14-ounce) racks of lamb	2	tablespoons Italian seasoning
½	cup Dijon mustard	1	tablespoon black pepper
1	cup breadcrumbs	1	cup Romano cheese

SAUCE

1	cup red wine	1	tablespoon chopped fresh rosemary
¼	cup roasted garlic, or to taste		Salt and pepper to taste
1	tablespoon rubbed sage	2	cups demi-glacé mix, prepared according to package
1	tablespoon sugar, or to taste		

Pan sear lamb and all sides. Brush lamb with mustard. Combine breadcrumbs, Italian seasoning, black pepper and cheese. Sprinkle breadcrumb mixture over lamb. Bake at 375° to desired degree of doneness, about 12 minutes for medium rare. To make sauce, combine wine, garlic, sage, sugar and rosemary in a saucepan. Season with salt and pepper. Cook until reduced to 1 cup. Add demi-glacé and simmer 5 minutes.

Yield: 4 to 6 servings

Blackened Tuna with Pineapple Black Bean Salsa

2	cups cooked black beans	½	cup pineapple juice
2	cups diced pineapple	¼	cup vinegar
½	cup diced red bell pepper	½	cup chopped parsley
½	cup diced yellow bell pepper		Salt and pepper to taste
¼	cup diced red onion	4-6	(7- to 8-ounce) tuna steaks
2	tablespoons chopped scallions	1	cup blackening spice
¼	cup chopped fresh thyme or cilantro		Sprigs of fresh cilantro for garnish

To prepare salsa, combine black beans, pineapple, bell peppers, onion, scallions, thyme, pineapple juice, vinegar and parsley in a mixing bowl. Season with salt and pepper and refrigerate at least 2 hours. When ready to serve, heat a cast iron pan over low heat for about 10 minutes. Dust tuna steaks with blackening spice. Sear steaks to desired degree of doneness. Serve tuna with salsa and garnish with cilantro.

Yield: 4 to 6 servings

Artwork by Jennifer Smith

Roast Tenderloin Roulade Filled with Steamed Lobster Meat and Spinach with Roasted Red Pepper Glaze

ROULADE

2½ pounds beef tenderloin
1 pound fresh spinach
½ pound raw lobster

1 tablespoon salt
1 tablespoon black pepper
1 tablespoon dried oregano

SAUCE

3 cups red wine
2 tablespoons rubbed sage
1 red bell pepper, roasted, skinned and
    chopped

1 tablespoon beef base
2 cups demi-glacé mix, prepared according
    to package
Salt and pepper to taste

Cut tenderloin to form a large, thin sheet. Steam spinach and lobster until lobster is about half cooked. Combine spinach, lobster, salt, pepper and oregano and spread over beef. Roll so as to resemble original shape of tenderloin. Sear all sides of beef over medium-high heat. Cut into 4 to 6 servings. Transfer to oven and bake at 375° until cooked to desired degree of doneness. To prepare sauce, combine red wine, sage, bell pepper and beef base in a medium saucepan. Cook over medium-high heat until reduced by half. Add demi-glacé and cook, uncovered, 10 minutes longer. Season with salt and pepper.

Yield: 4 to 6 servings

Pan Seared Stuffed Duck with Purple Plum Chutney

STUFFED DUCK

1	cup sliced shiitake mushrooms	1	tablespoon chicken base
1	cup oysters	¾	cup white wine
1	cup andouille sausage	1	cup breadcrumbs
	Salt and black pepper to taste	4-6	(5-ounce) duck breasts
1	teaspoon cayenne pepper		

SAUCE

12	purple plums, halved and seeded	1	cup vinegar
½	cup sliced red onion	½	cup honey
¼	cup sliced jalapeño pepper, or to taste		Salt and pepper to taste

Sauté mushrooms, oysters and sausage. Season with salt, black pepper, cayenne pepper and chicken base. Deglaze pan with wine. Simmer 7 to 8 minutes. Chill for one hour. Stir mixture into breadcrumbs. Make a small cut into each duck breast large enough to hold about ⅓ cup stuffing. Stuff each breast with breadcrumb mixture. Sear breasts, fatty-side down, over medium-high heat until crispy. Reduce to medium heat and turn breasts. Cook to desired degree of doneness. To prepare sauce, combine all ingredients in a large saucepan and bring to a boil. Cook until reduced to desired consistency.

Yield: 4 to 6 servings

Key Lime Pie

CRUST

4   cups graham cracker crumbs
1   stick unsalted butter, melted

½   cup sugar
Nonstick cooking spray

FILLING

6   egg yolks
1   cup key lime juice

2   (14-ounce) cans sweetened condensed milk

TOPPING

6   egg whites
1   teaspoon cream of tartar

1   cup sugar

To make crust, combine crumbs, butter and sugar. Pat mixture into a 9-inch pie pan coated with nonstick cooking spray. Bake at 300° for 10 minutes. Prepare filling by combining egg yolks, lime juice and milk in a bowl. Whisk thoroughly. Pour filling into prepared crust and bake 10 minutes at 350°, Chill 2 hours to allow filling to set. Meanwhile, prepare topping by combining sugar, cream of tartar and egg whites in a bowl. Let stand for 1 hour to dissolve sugar. Beat with an electric mixer on high for 10 minutes. Spread over top of pie. Bake at 375° for 5 minutes. Chill 30 minutes or until cool.

Yield: 8 servings

Christ Church

Delaney's
Bistro

Tom Delaney was born in Norwich, Connecticut, and has worked in restaurants since he was 17 years old. He graduated from Johnson and Wales University located in Providence, Rhode Island in 1984. After graduating he headed South to marry a local, and worked at Greyfield Inn, Riverwatch and Emmeline and Hessie, to name a few restaurants in the area.

In the spring of 1994, Chef Tom opened his own restaurant, Delaney's Bistro where he enjoys catering to locals and visitors alike. Some of his signature dishes include Grilled Magret Duck Breast with a Tai Peanut Sauce, Charred Fresh Foie Gras Verjus, and a variety of fresh seafood and game dishes.

Since Delaney's opened, it has been called the best kept secret on Saint Simon's Island. It has an intimate, fine dining atmosphere and is located on the north end of the Island.

Tomato-Crab Bisque

1	(28-ounce) can diced tomatoes	2	cups chicken broth
1	small Spanish onion, finely diced	¼	cup dry sherry
4	tablespoons butter		Salt and white pepper to taste
½	cup flour	8	ounces blue crab claw meat
1½	quarts half-and-half		

Combine tomato and onion in a small saucepan and simmer 5 minutes. Whisk butter and flour in a medium saucepan over medium heat. Slowly add half-and-half. Whisk until sauce is smooth and simmering. Add chicken broth. Stir in tomato mixture. Cook 10 minutes, stirring frequently to avoid scorching. Bisque can be pureed at this point if a smoother texture is desired. Add sherry and season with salt and pepper. Fold crab meat into soup and serve.

Yield: 6 to 8 servings

I like it with chunks of tomatoes and Tom likes his pureed.

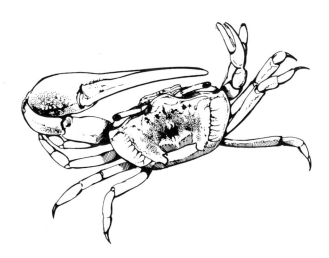

Artwork by Jennifer Smith

Escargots Roquefort

32 extra large snails
1½ cups heavy cream
½ cup white wine

1 cup Roquefort cheese
Salt and pepper to taste

Combine heavy cream and wine in saucepan. Bring to a boil and reduce until thickened. Add Roquefort cheese, salt and pepper to taste. Serve with or in toasted French bread.

Yield: 4 servings

Artwork by Jennifer Smith

Portobella Mushroom Pizza

1	(4-inch diameter) portobella mushroom, stem removed
1	tablespoon extra virgin olive oil
1	tablespoon chopped mixed fresh herbs (oregano, parsley, or basil)
	Granulated garlic to taste
	Black pepper to taste
¼	cup diced tomato
¼	cup sliced scallions
2	ounces Montrachet cheese
¼	cup grated mozzarella cheese
¼	cup shredded Parmesan cheese

With bottom of mushroom cap facing up, score the dense center 4 to 5 times. Lightly brush olive oil over the center and surrounding ribs and sprinkle with herbs. Season with garlic and black pepper. Sprinkle tomato and scallions over mushroom cap. Crumble Montrachet cheese evenly on top. Add mozzarella cheese and place on a baking pan. Bake at 425° for about 6 to 7 minutes. Dust with Parmesan cheese and bake 2 minutes longer or until golden and bubbly. Slice into 6 pieces and serve on a warm plate.

Yield: 1 serving

Eggplant and Buffalo Mozzarella Napoleon

MARINARA SAUCE

1	tablespoon olive oil		2	teaspoons Italian seasoning
¼	cup diced white onion		1	(14.5-ounce) can diced tomatoes
¼	cup diced carrot			Salt and pepper to taste

NAPOLEON

1	loaf French bread		1	medium eggplant, cut into
½	cup Parmesan cheese			8 (¾-inch) slices
2	teaspoons Italian seasoning		3	tablespoons olive oil, divided
1	cup flour		4	(¼-inch) thick slices tomato
4	eggs, beaten		4	(1½-inch) thick slices Buffalo mozzarella
				Fresh basil for garnish

Heat a medium saucepan with olive oil. Add onion and carrot and sauté 2 to 3 minutes without browning. Add Italian seasoning and tomatoes and bring to a simmer. Cook about 10 minutes. Season with salt and pepper. Meanwhile, prepare Napoleon by processing bread in a food processor to form very fine breadcrumbs. Combine breadcrumbs, Parmesan cheese and Italian seasoning in a shallow dish. Place flour and egg in 2 separate shallow dishes. Dip the eggplant in flour and shake off any excess. Dip in egg and then coat with breadcrumb mixture. Sauté the eggplant in 2 batches, using 1½ tablespoons olive oil per batch. Cook over medium-low heat until golden brown. Layer eggplant with tomato slices and mozzarella slices and season with salt and pepper. Cook 30 seconds on each side. Arrange 4 slices of eggplant on a baking sheet. Top with a tomato slice, a slice of mozzarella and another slice of eggplant. Bake at 400° for about 7 minutes. To serve, spoon 3 ounces of sauce onto individual plates. Place Napoleon on top. Garnish with fresh basil.

Yield: 4 servings

Poached Salmon Chambord

2	cups Chardonnay or dry white wine		1	tablespoon fresh lemon juice
4	cups water		1	teaspoon kosher salt
½	teaspoon black peppercorns		¾	cup Merlot or Zinfandel
	Dill to taste		¼	cup Chambord liqueur
	Thyme to taste		1	teaspoon cornstarch
	Fennel seed to taste		¾	cup sliced shiitake mushrooms
4	(6- to 8-ounce) salmon fillets			Kosher salt and freshly ground pepper to taste

Place Chardonnay, water, peppercorns, dill, thyme and fennel in a large baking pan. Bring to a boil over medium heat. Simmer 3 minutes. Meanwhile, rub fillets with lemon juice and sprinkle with salt. Let stand 2 minutes and then transfer fillets, in a single layer, to baking pan. Return Chardonnay broth to a simmer and cook 3 minutes per inch fillet thickness. Do not allow broth to boil rapidly. Meanwhile, add Merlot to a saucepan over medium heat. In a separate container, whisk together Chambord and cornstarch until smooth. Add to Merlot and whisk constantly until thickened and smooth. Season mushrooms with salt and pepper and sauté in a skillet. To serve, pour Merlot sauce onto a platter. Arrange fillets on platter and top with mushrooms.

Yield: 4 servings

Fillet of Beef Béarnaise

4	(8-ounce) beef fillets	1	tablespoon chopped fresh tarragon, or
	Kosher salt and freshly cracked black		2 teaspoons dry
	pepper to taste	2	egg yolks
1	small shallot, minced	1	teaspoon Dijon mustard
¼	cup white wine vinegar	3	sticks butter, melted and kept warm
¼	cup white wine		

Season fillets with salt and pepper. Sear over high heat on a grill or in a pan. Reduce heat or in the case of pan searing, place in a 350° oven, and cook to desired degree of doneness. To make béarnaise sauce, place shallot, vinegar, wine and tarragon in a small saucepan. Cook until reduced by half then cool. Place yolks in a bowl and whisk with mustard and 2 pinches of salt. Add cooled wine reduction and cook over a double boiler, whisking constantly until mixture thickens enough to form a ribbon-like pattern on surface when dropped from the whisk. Remove from heat and slowly stir in butter, except for the whey, until smooth. Season with salt and pepper. Place each fillet on a serving plate and top with béarnaise sauce.

Yield: 4 servings

Snapper Hemingway

SNAPPER

4   (8-ounce) snapper fillets
½   cup flour
    Juice of 1 lemon
    Salt to taste

½   cup sesame seeds
    Butter for sautéing
    Water or wine for baking

LEMON BLANC SAUCE

1   cup heavy cream
6   tablespoons lemon juice

4   tablespoons butter, quartered

Dredge snapper in flour, then rub with lemon juice. Season with salt and dip in sesame seeds. Sauté in butter in a skillet until brown on one side. Add water or wine to cover bottom of skillet and bake at 450° for about 8 minutes. Meanwhile, prepare sauce by combining cream and lemon juice in a saucepan. Bring to a boil and reduce until thickened. Remove from heat, add butter and whisk until smooth. Transfer baked fish to individual plates. Pour sauce over fish and serve.

Yield: 4 servings

Veal Michelangelo

3	(3-ounce) veal leg cutlets	3	tablespoons fresh lemon juice
¼	teaspoon salt or to taste	1	teaspoon chopped shallots
¼	teaspoon white pepper or to taste	3	tablespoons heavy cream
¼	teaspoon thyme leaves	4	tablespoons unsalted butter, quartered
2	eggs, beaten	2	canned artichoke hearts, halved
1½	teaspoons clarified butter	2	slices ripe avocado
¼	cup flour	¼	cup Parmesan cheese

Using a mallet, a cleaver, or the bottom of a heavy pan, flatten veal cutlets between plastic wrap to ¹⁄₁₆-inch thick. Season with salt, pepper and thyme. Combine egg with a tablespoon of water in a shallow dish. Heat clarified butter in a nonstick skillet over medium-high heat. Dredge cutlets in flour, shaking off any excess. Dip in egg wash and transfer cutlets to heated skillet. Cook about 1 minute on each side. Remove from skillet and keep warm. Pour lemon juice into skillet. Add shallots and cream and boil until reduced by half. Remove from heat, add unsalted butter and whisk until smooth. Shingle the cutlets, artichoke hearts and avocado slices on a serving plate. Dust with Parmesan cheese and place in a hot oven for 1 minute. Drizzle with lemon sauce and serve.

Yield: 1 serving

Veal Hannah

VEAL

12	veal cutlets	3	tablespoons butter, divided
	Salt and pepper to taste	1	cup flour
3	eggs, beaten	8	ounces mushrooms, sliced

SAUCE

1	cup heavy cream	4	ounces crabmeat, flaked
2	tablespoons dry sherry		

Flatten cutlets between plastic wrap using a mallet or cleaver. Season with salt and pepper. Combine egg and 2 tablespoons water in a flat dish. Heat 2 tablespoons butter in a skillet. Dredge cutlets in flour, shaking off excess. Dip in egg wash and transfer to heated skillet. Sauté until golden brown. Transfer to a serving platter. Sauté mushrooms in remaining tablespoon of butter in a saucepan. Sprinkle mushrooms over veal. To prepare sauce, add cream, sherry and crabmeat to saucepan and bring to a boil. Pour sauce over veal and serve.

Yield: 4 to 6 servings

Creamy Polenta

4	cups chicken broth	¾	cup medium-grain polenta
¼	cup diced sun-dried tomatoes	½	cup sour cream
1	clove garlic, pressed	½	cup Parmesan cheese
1	tablespoon dried Italian herbs		

Bring chicken broth to a boil in a saucepan. Add tomatoes, garlic, and herbs and boil for 1 minute. Whisk in polenta, stirring constantly, until smooth. Reduce to a simmer and cook 20 minutes, stirring frequently. Remove from heat and stir in sour cream and cheese.

Yield: 4 to 6 servings

Baked Tomatoes

4	tomatoes, cored and halved	½	cup breadcrumbs
1	stick butter, melted, divided	½	cup Parmesan cheese
	Salt and pepper to taste	2	tablespoons dried Italian herbs

Place tomatoes in a baking dish, cut side up, and brush with some of melted butter. Season with salt and pepper. Sprinkle breadcrumbs, cheese, and herbs on top. Drizzle with remaining butter. Bake at 425° until topping is lightly browned.

Yield: 4 servings

Tiramisu Torte

CAKE

1 teaspoon plus 2 tablespoons unsalted
      butter, melted, divided
2 teaspoons plus ½ cup flour, divided
3 eggs
3 egg yolks

½ cup granulated sugar
1 teaspoon vanilla
3 egg whites
3 tablespoons cornstarch

ICING AND TOPPING

1 pound mascarpone cheese
8 ounces cream cheese
3 cups powdered sugar
3 ounces amaretto

3 ounces coffee liqueur
1 cup slivered almonds, toasted
¾ cup grated semisweet chocolate

Brush 1 teaspoon butter in a 9-inch cake pan. Dust pan with 2 teaspoons flour. Using an electric mixer, whip eggs, yolks and sugar at high speed for 5 minutes or until thickened and lemon colored. Add vanilla and whip 1 minute. Using a clean bowl and beaters, whip egg whites 2 minutes or until soft peaks form. Sift cornstarch and remaining flour into egg yolk batter. Gently fold into batter using a rubber spatula. Fold egg white and remaining butter into batter. Pour mixture into cake pan. Bake at 350° for 17 minutes. Remove from oven and cool 10 minutes. Turn out of pan and cool 30 minutes longer. To make icing, use an electric mixer to combine cheeses and sugar until smooth. To assemble torte, use a serrated knife to split cake in half, forming 2 circles. Drizzle halves with amaretto and liqueur. Frost the bottom layer of the torte. Place remaining layer on top and frost the top and sides. Press almonds onto the sides of the torte and sprinkle chocolate over the top.

Yield: 12 servings

Strawberries with Champagne Sabayon

2   pints strawberries, stemmed, rinsed and drained
3   egg yolks
½   cup sugar

½   cup champagne
¼   cup Cointreau
     Pinch of sugar

Place 1½ inches of water in a saucepan and bring to a boil over high heat. Place egg yolks, ½ cup sugar and champagne in a stainless steel mixing bowl. Whisk to combine. Place bowl over boiling water and whisk constantly for 5 to 7 minutes or until thickened and glossy. Do not undercook. Remove from heat and whisk in Cointreau. Sprinkle strawberries with a pinch of sugar and toss. Arrange strawberries on a serving platter. Pour sauce in a small bowl for dipping.

HALYARDS

Pork and Shrimp Pot Stickers,
page 50

Endive Salad,
page 52

Red Pepper Pesto Snapper
with Balsamic Butter, Spinach, and Pancetta,
page 55

Seared Beef Tenderloin with Buttermilk
Mashed Potatoes, Asparagus, and Bordelaise,
page 56

Banana Nut Bread Pudding,
page 59

Halyards is the dream-come-true of Dave Snyder and Bryan Sibley. Opened in February of 2000, a great staff and environment have enabled Halyards to begin with great success. Dinner offers contemporary American cuisine, an alternative wine list, and fun, efficient service.

Dave Snyder graduated from the New England Culinary Institute with experience in various restaurants and hotels. After working with Les Celebrities, Union Square Café, Zoe, and The Mark, he moved his career to the South. Before Halyards, he was the chef at Azalea in Atlanta and J Mac's.

Bryan Sibley attained his BPS from the Culinary Institute of America and experience from great Southern establishments. His career has taken him from Pano's & Paul's in Atlanta to Highlands Bar & Grill in Birmingham. As co-owner, Bryan orchestrates the staff in the dining room and enables the guests to feel like family.

Pork and Shrimp Pot Stickers

1	pound pork, ground		1	teaspoon cayenne pepper
1	pound shrimp, ground			Salt and pepper to taste
1	tablespoon miso paste			Wonton skins
1	tablespoon fish sauce			Vegetable oil
2	tablespoons chopped fresh cilantro			Soy sauce and diagonally sliced scallions
1	bunch scallions, minced			for garnish

Combine pork, shrimp, miso, fish sauce, cilantro, minced scallions and cayenne pepper. Season with salt and pepper. Wrap mixture in wonton skins. Sear over high heat in a small amount of hot vegetable oil. Reduce heat to medium-low and turn pot stickers as they brown. Add water to cover bottom of pan and increase heat to high. Cover pan and steam for 1 minute. Transfer pot stickers to a serving plate using a slotted spoon. Garnish with soy sauce and scallions.

Endive Salad

SALAD

1	head Belgium endive, julienned	1	teaspoon minced shallots
1	ounce baby greens	½	teaspoon chopped fresh parsley
½	Granny Smith apple, sliced	1	tablespoon crumbled Gorgonzola cheese
1	tablespoon walnuts, toasted		Salt and pepper to taste
1	tablespoon diced tomatoes		

RASPBERRY VINAIGRETTE

1	cup raspberry vinegar	Salt and pepper to taste
3	cups blended olive oil	

Toss together all salad ingredients. In a separate container, mix vinaigrette ingredients. Add vinaigrette to salad to taste and toss. Serve on chilled plates.

Red Pepper Pesto Snapper with Balsamic Butter, Spinach, and Pancetta

RED PEPPER PESTO

2　cups roasted and peeled red peppers
2　cloves garlic, peeled
1　bunch basil, picked over
2　tablespoons pignoli, toasted

1　tablespoon grated Parmesan cheese
　　Salt and pepper to taste
　　Cayenne pepper to taste
　　Extra virgin olive oil

BALSAMIC BUTTER SAUCE

1　cup balsamic vinegar
2　sticks butter, cold and diced

　　Salt and pepper to taste

SNAPPER

1　(7 ounce) snapper fillet
　　Salt and pepper to taste
　　Olive oil
1　tablespoon sliced pancetta

2　cups fresh spinach, washed and stemmed
¼　cup Balsamic Butter Sauce
1　tablespoon Red Pepper Pesto

To make pesto, combine peppers, garlic, basil, pignoli, and cheese in a food processor. Process until coarsely chopped. Season with salt, pepper, cayenne pepper, and olive oil. To prepare butter sauce, reduce vinegar to a syrup consistency. Remove from heat and whip in cold butter. Season with salt and pepper. When ready to serve, season snapper with salt and pepper. Heat olive oil in a skillet for 10 seconds. Add snapper and saute until golden brown. Turn and transfer to a 400° oven. Bake 3 minutes or until done. In a separate skillet, saute pancetta for 3 to 5 minutes. Add spinach and saute over medium heat until spinach is tender. To serve, cover the bottom of a plate with butter sauce. Spoon spinach and pancetta into the center of the plate. Place snapper on top. Garnish with pesto.

Seared Beef Tenderloin with Buttermilk Mashed Potatoes, Asparagus, and Bordelaise

BEEF TENDERLOIN

1   (10 ounce) beef tenderloin steak
1   ounce Gorgonzola cheese
    Salt and pepper to taste
4   tablespoons butter
8   spears asparagus

Peeled, seeded, and chopped tomatoes
Chopped fresh parsley
Buttermilk mashed potatoes (use your
    favorite recipe)
2   ounces Bordelaise

BORDELAISE

2   cups Cabernet Sauvignon
1   shallot, sliced
1   bay leaf
1   sprig fresh thyme

1   sprig fresh parsley
1   cup demi-glace
    Salt and pepper to taste

Cut a pocket in steak and fill with cheese. Season with salt and pepper. Sear steak on one side in a hot pan. Turn steak and top with butter. Roast at 500° to desired temperature. Blanch asparagus and season to taste. Add tomatoes and parsley to asparagus and toss. Serve steak with asparagus mixture and mashed potatoes. Top steak with Bordelaise. To make Bordelaise, combine wine, shallot, bay leaf, thyme, and parsley in a saucepan. Cook over medium-high heat until reduced by half. Add demi-glace; strain. Season with salt and pepper.

Banana Nut Bread Pudding

PUDDING

6	cups breadcrumbs
4	eggs
3	sticks butter, melted
1	tablespoon vanilla
2	cups cream

½	cup brown sugar
½	cup granulated sugar
3	cups pureed banana
1	cup chopped pecans

SAUCE

2	cups cream cheese, room temperature
1	cup sour cream, room temperature

1	tablespoon vanilla

Combine all pudding ingredients except pecans in a mixing bowl. Add pecans and mix well. Pour mixture into a greased baking dish. Bake at 350° in a water bath for 40 minutes. To make sauce, mix together cheese, cream, and vanilla. Serve on top of pudding. Garnish with your favorite fruit and whipped cream.

Fort Frederica

CAFÉ FREDERICA

Café Frederica opened in June of 1987 serving from one menu where customers could choose either breakfast or lunch items—it worked. Several years later we expanded to our present size and have become a local's favorite. Most items on the menu are prepared in our open kitchen including biscuits, cinnamon rolls, soups and a variety of salads. We make our own Key Lime, Coconut Cream and Chocolate French Silk pies.

Over the last twelve years we have employed many young men and women to work in our restaurant to provide quality food and service. The cafe has a warm and friendly atmosphere and is nicely decorated to reflect the owner's interests. Note the Elvis alcove and the electric trains that run overhead. Please stop and visit. We are open 7 days a week from 7:30 a.m. to 2:00 p.m.

Cinnamon Rolls
A favorite at the Café; we've sold thousands.

1	(16-ounce) box soft roll mix	1	cup cinnamon
3	sticks margarine, melted	1	pound powdered sugar
2	cups granulated sugar		

Prepare soft roll mix according to package instructions. Roll out dough to ¼-inch thickness. Spread melted margarine over entire surface. Sprinkle generously with granulated sugar and cinnamon. Roll dough into a log and cut crosswise into 1½-inch sections. Place rolls, cut-side up, ½-inch apart on a greased baking sheet. Cover lightly and allow to rise until rolls are large and fluffy. Bake at 350° until light brown. To prepare a glaze, combine powdered sugar with a small amount of water until smooth and spreadable. Spread liberally over rolls. Serve warm.

Roast Beef Hash

**A quick cut from the original, born out of necessity
one morning in 1988. A great breakfast item.**

¼   red onion, chopped
18   small red bliss potatoes, cooked and
     chopped

Butter for sautéing
Mrs. Dash seasoning to taste
½   pound cooked roast beef, chopped

Sauté onion and potato in butter until browned. Season with Mrs. Dash. Add beef and sauté until hot.

Yield: 2 servings

Boz Bagel

**Developed by a friend of mine, Father Goose.
A good morning start with a cup of our fresh ground coffee.**

1   plain bagel
     Cream cheese

Sliced tomato
Chopped red onion

Toast bagel. Top with cream cheese, tomato and onion.

Yield: 1 serving

Eggs Benedict

A Café favorite. We use a Knorr Swiss product and add some lemon juice and Tabasco to make a Hollandaise sauce. At home, use the recipe below.

4	egg yolks		2	English muffins, halved
¼	cup butter or margarine, melted		4	(1- to 2-ounce) slices Georgia smoked ham
1	tablespoon lemon juice, or to taste		2-4	eggs

To prepare Hollandaise sauce, place egg yolks in a saucepan over a double boiler and beat. Gradually whisk in butter and lemon juice and cook about 2 minutes. Do not overcook or the sauce will break down. Meanwhile, toast English muffin halves and place on serving plates. Grill ham until warm and lay over halves. Poach eggs and place on top of ham. Add Hollandaise sauce and serve with fruit slices.

Yield: 2 servings

Artwork by Jennifer Smith

Creamed Chipped Beef

This has been a favorite here at the Café. The only complaint is that we sometimes serve too much.

2 tablespoons butter	2 tablespoons sour cream
2 tablespoons flour	3 cups dried chipped beef
2 cups milk	White pepper to taste

Melt butter in a saucepan. Stir in flour until smooth and cook until bubbly. Slowly stir in milk and cook until thick and smooth. Remove from heat and stir in sour cream and beef. Season with pepper. Serve over toasted English muffins, hot biscuits, or toast.

Yield: 1 to 2 servings

Sausage and Potato Soup

Over the years, we have had many good cooks. Once in a while, one of them will come up with a great soup or sandwich. Here is one that Steve Ebert, a great cook who came to us from a resort in Colorado, came up with. It has been a Café favorite.

1	pound fresh sausage, chopped
1	small onion, diced
1	stalk celery, diced
2	tablespoons oil
8-10	red bliss potatoes, peeled and cut into 1-inch cubes
⅓	cup flour

1	quart heavy cream
1	quart chicken broth
½	teaspoon Worcestershire sauce
⅛	teaspoon Tabasco sauce
1	teaspoon Mrs. Dash seasoning
½	teaspoon granulated garlic
	White pepper to taste

Sauté sausage, onion and celery in oil. Add potato and stir until coated with oil. Stir in flour until a thick paste forms. Add cream, broth, Worcestershire sauce, Tabasco sauce, Mrs. Dash, garlic and white pepper. Simmer on low to medium-low heat, stirring constantly with a spoon. Do not use a wire whip. Soup is ready when the potato is tender and the liquid coats a metal spoon.

Yield: 2 to 4 servings

Caesar Salad Dressing

6	eggs	2	tablespoons Worcestershire sauce
3	tablespoons Dijon mustard	1	cup Parmesan cheese
1½	tablespoons chopped garlic	1	quart olive oil
¾	cup red wine vinegar		Salt and pepper to taste

Whisk together eggs, mustard, garlic, vinegar, Worcestershire sauce and cheese. Whisk in oil slowly in a steady stream. Season with salt and pepper.

Yield: 1½ quarts

Café Shrimp Salad

Our shrimp salad is served on a bed of greens with a side of pasta. A great lunch. We buy our shrimp already peeled and deveined from Red at The City Market.

	Old Bay seasoning to taste	Chopped celery to taste
2-3	pounds peeled and deveined medium shrimp	Celery Seed to taste
		Mayonnaise to taste

Add Old Bay seasoning to a large pot of water and bring to a boil. Stir in shrimp and cook a few minutes until done. Be careful not to overcook. Drain and cool shrimp. Combine shrimp with celery, celery seed and mayonnaise.

Yield: 6 to 8 servings

Pier at Saint Simon's

Low Country Favorites

Broiled Parmesan Cheese Oysters,
page 76

Seafood Gumbo,
page 76

Brunswick Stew,
page 77

Low Country Boil,
page 78

Crabmeat Stuffed Flounder,
page 80

Sauté Soft Shell Crabs with
Lemon Butter Sauce,
page 82

Shrimp and Scallop Alfredo,
page 84

Shrimp Mull,
page 84

Fried Shrimp and Gravy,
page 86

Grandpa Turner's Vinaigrette Slaw,
page 86

Boiled Blue Crabs,
page 88

Low Country Favorites

Broiled Parmesan Cheese Oysters

1	pint oyster selects		1	tablespoon Old Bay seasoning
4	tablespoons butter, melted		¼	cup Parmesan cheese
	Chopped garlic to taste			Salt and pepper to taste

Lay oysters on a broiler pan. Combine butter and garlic. Brush oysters with garlic butter and sprinkle with Old Bay seasoning, cheese, salt and pepper. Broil 5 to 6 minutes or until done.

Yield: 2 to 4 servings

Seafood Gumbo

1	onion, chopped		½	pound shrimp, peeled and deveined
1	red bell pepper, chopped		½	pound fresh fish
1	green bell pepper, chopped		1	(6½-ounce) can chopped clams
1	stalk celery, chopped		1	cup chopped tasso or sausage
1	tablespoon chopped garlic		½	(16-ounce) bag frozen okra
1	stick butter		1	teaspoon thyme
½	cup flour		1	teaspoon Old Bay seasoning
8	cups broth			Salt and pepper to taste
1	(28-ounce) can diced tomatoes			

In a large pot, sauté onion, bell peppers, celery and garlic in butter until tender. Add flour and cook and stir to form a brown roux. Add broth and tomatoes. Simmer 20 minutes. Add shrimp, fish, clams, tasso, okra, thyme and Old Bay seasoning. Cook, stirring occasionally, until seafood is cooked. Season with salt and pepper. Serve over rice.

Yield: 6 to 8 servings

Brunswick Stew

6	chicken (white meat) quarters	1	bottle chili sauce
1	pound round steak	2	teaspoons dry mustard
2	pounds lean pork	3	tablespoons vinegar
2	medium onions, diced	1	bag frozen small butter beans
4	cans diced tomatoes	1	can cream white corn
5	tablespoons Worcestershire sauce	1	can whole corn
2	bottles catsup	1	bag frozen English peas
4	teaspoons Tabasco sauce	3	diced potatoes
4	bay leaves		Salt and pepper to taste

Put meat in a large pot. Cover with water. Cook until meat falls off bones. Allow to cool. Remove meat from bones and shred. Drain stock and defat by cooling in refrigerator. Add onions, tomatoes, Worcestershire sauce, catsup, Tabasco, bay leaves, chili sauce and dry mustard. Cook for 1 hour, stirring to prevent sticking. Add the remaining ingredients and cook on low until done, about 1 hour.

Yield: 15 servings

Low Country Boil

½ cup Old Bay seasoning
½ lemon
12-16 new potatoes
8 small onions
6 ears of corn, halved

2 pounds kielbasa sausage
3 pounds medium to large shrimp in their
shells
Salt and pepper to taste

Fill a 12-quart pot half full with water. Bring to a boil. Add Old Bay seasoning and lemon. Add potatoes and onions and boil 10 minutes. Add corn and sausage and boil 10 minutes longer. Reduce heat to a simmer and add shrimp. Cook until shrimp are done and potatoes are tender. Season with salt and pepper. Serve with melted butter and cocktail sauce.

Yield: 6 to 8 servings

Artwork by Jennifer Smith

Crabmeat Stuffed Flounder

STUFFING

1   stick butter
½   red bell pepper, diced
½   green bell pepper, diced
1   yellow onion, diced
1   stalk celery, diced
1   tablespoon Old Bay seasoning
1   teaspoon dry mustard

1   teaspoon thyme
½   teaspoon black pepper
⅓   cup flour
1   cup half-and-half
1   tablespoon Worcestershire sauce
1   pound blue crab claw meat, picked over

FLOUNDER

6   (6- to 8-ounce) boneless flounder fillets
½   cup fresh lemon juice
    Salt and white pepper to taste
½   cup fresh French breadcrumbs

4   tablespoons butter, melted
½   cup dry white wine
½   cup water

To make stuffing, melt butter in a medium saucepan. Add bell peppers, onion, celery, Old Bay seasoning, mustard, thyme and black pepper. Cook over medium heat for 3 minutes. Stir in flour until smooth. Mix in half-and-half and Worcestershire sauce. Cook 2 minutes, stirring constantly. Remove from heat and let cool 5 minutes. Carefully fold in crabmeat. To prepare flounder, carefully trim away any small bones from the thick end of the fillets. Gently remove any ribbed meat that may encircle the fillets. Using a sharp paring knife, score the fillets lengthwise in the seam of the meat starting 1 inch from the top and ending 1 inch from the bottom. Divide stuffing into six equal portions, evenly spacing them on a greased baking sheet. Place fillets over the stuffing, opening the cut center to form a window to expose some of the stuffing. Shape stuffing to form a high point in the center and to allow fillets to cling to the pan all around the stuffing. Drizzle fillets with lemon juice and season with salt and pepper. Lightly sprinkle breadcrumbs over fillets and drizzle with butter. Pour wine and water into the pan. Bake at 425° for 12 minutes.

Yield: 6 servings

Sauté Soft Shell Crabs with Lemon Butter Sauce

CRABS

2	eggs
1	cup milk
1	cup flour
1	tablespoon Old Bay seasoning

	Salt and pepper to taste
8	medium soft shell crabs
¼	cup oil
4	tablespoons butter

LEMON BUTTER SAUCE

1	cup heavy cream
	Juice of 1 lemon
1	stick butter

Salt to taste
Chopped parsley

Beat eggs and milk together. Combine flour, Old Bay seasoning, salt and pepper in a shallow pan. Soak crabs in egg mixture for about 2 minutes. Dip in flour mixture. Combine oil and butter in a skillet over medium heat. Add crabs and sauté until golden brown on both sides. Serve with Lemon Butter Sauce. To make sauce, bring cream to a boil in a saucepan. Remove from heat and whip in lemon juice, butter, salt and parsley.

Yield: 4 servings

Shrimp and Scallop Alfredo

1	pound shrimp, peeled and deveined	½	cup grated Parmesan cheese
1	pound scallops	2	teaspoons chopped garlic
4	tablespoons butter	1	(16-ounce) package pasta, cooked al dente
2	cups heavy cream		Salt and pepper to taste
1	red bell pepper, thinly sliced	½	cup shredded Parmesan cheese

In a large skillet, sauté shrimp and scallops in butter over medium heat until light pink. Stir in cream and simmer until bubbly. Add bell pepper, grated Parmesan cheese, garlic and pasta. Toss gently and season with salt and pepper. Sprinkle with shredded Parmesan cheese and serve.

Yield: 4 servings

Shrimp Mull

8	slices bacon, diced	6	cups broth
1	onion, diced	2	pounds shrimp, peeled and deveined
6	baking potatoes, diced		Salt and pepper to taste

Sauté bacon until brown. Add onion and sauté until tender. Add potato and broth and cook until potatoes are al dente. Stir in shrimp and simmer until done. Season to taste with salt and pepper. Tastes best served with cornbread.

Yield: 4 servings

Fried Shrimp and Gravy

1½ pounds shrimp, peeled and deveined
Salt and pepper to taste
¾ cup flour
½ cup yellow cornmeal
½ cup olive oil, divided
1 onion, diced

1 red bell pepper, diced
1 green bell pepper, diced
1 tablespoon chopped garlic
1 cup chopped tasso
4 cups broth
Hot pepper sauce to taste

Season shrimp with salt and pepper. Dust with flour and cornmeal, shaking off excess. Reserve flour for later use. Heat oil in a skillet. Add shrimp and sauté until light brown. Remove shrimp, leaving oil in pan. Add onion, bell peppers, garlic and tasso to pan and sauté until vegetables are tender. Dust vegetables with reserved flour. Stir in broth and cook to make a thick sauce. Add shrimp and cook 1 minute. Season with salt, pepper and hot pepper sauce. Serve with rice or polenta.

Yield: 4 servings

Grandpa Turner's Vinaigrette Slaw

8 slices bacon, diced
¾ cup apple cider vinegar
¼ cup water

1 small heat cabbage, shredded
Salt and pepper to taste
1 small onion, thinly sliced

Sauté bacon in a skillet until brown. Cool. Stir in vinegar and water. Season cabbage with salt and pepper. Combine cabbage, onion and vinegar mixture. Toss and serve.

Yield: 8 servings

Boiled Blue Crabs

½ cup Old Bay seasoning
1 lemon, halved
Dash of hot pepper sauce

2 bay leaves
1 dozen fresh crabs

Fill a large pot half full with water. Bring to a boil. Add Old Bay seasoning, lemon, hot pepper sauce and bay leaves. Add crabs and cook until red. Serve with melted butter and cocktail sauce.

Acknowledgments

Thanks to all the people for their assistance
in the production and faith of this book.

Restaurants and their staffs

John Toth and his staff at the Darkroom

Our good friends Chuck and B.J. Egland at St. Simon's Seafood

Our local Artists:
Paul Patterson
Karen Keene
Mildred Huie
Jennifer Smith

Our good friend Fran Newton

Worldone Computors for all their help

Our wonderful families for being patient

And last but not least thanks to all the local
support of our restaurants and for the interest in this cookbook.

Acknowledgments

David McKim

Thanks to David McKim who brought to the cookbook *Low Country Favorites* and will be a great partner on many future projects. This cookbook would not have been completed without his persistence and hard work.

Paul Patterson

Paul Patterson, professional artist, is a native of Georgia. On the island of St. Simon's he grew up to a way of life that influenced the growth of his natural talent as an artist. With the guidance of his grandmother, the renowned artist Stella Morton, this natural artist advanced his techniques and skills with the various media at an early age. Though he received no actual formal art training, the notice of his superb draftsmanship resulted in his artwork being featured in school publications throughout his high school and college years.

Long noted for his strength of composition and subtle colors, Paul Patterson is at his finest in depicting the serene majesty of his native Georgia coast. Seeing the area through the eyes of an artist of Patterson's caliber is a rewarding and unforgettable experience.

Left Bank Art Gallery

Mildred Huie, noted Saint Simon's artist is also one of the most important historians of Coastal Georgia. *The Ruins of Fort Frederica* is from the series of *Georgia's Coastal Landmarks* which also include *The Avenue of Oaks*, *The Cloister Lily Pond*, *The Marshes of Glynn*, *Christ Church*, *Hopeton Plantation*, and *Boats at the Sea Island Docks*.

This collection is available as originals, prints or as art cards and can be seen at Left Bank Art Gallery, 3600 Frederica Road, Suite 12 or call 912-638-3017 or 1-800-336-9469. The Gallery is open Tuesday-Saturday from 10 a.m. to 5 p.m.

Karen Keene Braswell

Karen Keene Braswell is an award-winning academically trained artist who resides on St. Simons Island. She jokingly calls herself a "Hoosier by birth and Bulldog by Grace of God".
"I had three outstanding art professors, Glenn Chesnutt at MGC, Lamar Dodd at UGA and Bill Hendrix at the Coastal Center for the Arts."

Art is a family affair . . . husband Rance Braswell, owner of Commonwealth Realty, is responsible for marketing and promotion. The blue crabs that daughter Martha caught at the pier and migrating butterflies became the inspiration for "crablet" and "flutterby" prints. The "Shells by the Inch" series was inspired by beach finds and "Other Fish in the Sea" series was inspired by Martha catching a flounder in her crab net.

Karen's numerous Limited Edition reproductions of local and regional landmarks capture the natural beauty of Georgia's Colonial Coast and are painted on location. Her nature prints are available in fine gift shops and art galleries along the Eastern seaboard and Gulf Coast.

Index

D

Desserts

E

Eggplant

Eggs

F

Fish

G

Game

L

Lamb

M

P

Pasta